# Portraits

Wolfgang Tillmans

# List of Plates

| | *person, city* | *title, year* |
|---|---|---|
| 1 | **Irm Hermann**, Munich | *Irm Hermann*, 2000 |
| 2 | **Valerie Villaume**, London | *Valerie Villaume*, 2000 |
| 3 | **Richard James**, London | *Richard James*, 2001 |
| 4 | **Richard James**, London | *Aphex, looking up*, 2001 |
| 5 | **Markus Krottendorfer**, Vienna | *Markus in Gasometer*, 1998 |
| 6 | **Andre Weisheit**, Munich | *tightrope*, 2000 |
| 7 | **Billie Ray Martin**, Munich | *Billie Ray Martin*, 1999 |
| 8 | **Moby**, London | *Moby (lying)*, 1993 |
| 9 | **Hedi Slimane**, London | *Hedi Slimane*, 2000 |
| 10 | **Volker Antenreiter**, London | *Volker, standing*, 2000 |
| 11 | **Jochen Klein**, London | *Jochen in Viet Hoa*, 1997 |
| 12 | **Jason Evans**, London | *Jason Evans*, 2000 |
| 13 | **Wolfgang Tillmans**, Lucca | *nothing to loose*, 1997 |
| 14 | **Morwenna Banks**, New York | *Morwenna Banks, mirror*, 1995 |
| 15 | **Grandmaster Flash**, New York | *Grandmaster Flash, mirrors*, 1995 |
| 16 | **Jarvis Cocker**, London | *Jarvis Cocker*, 1998 |
| 17 | **Michael Clark**, Lucca | *Michael Clark*, 1998 |
| 18 | **Chris Cunningham**, London | *Chris Cunningham*, 1998 |
| 19 | **Vidya Gastaldon**, Lucca | *Vidya*, 1999 |
| 20 | **Chloe Sevigny**, New York | *Chloe*, 1995 |
| 21 | **Steve Slocombe**, London | *Steve*, 1999 |
| 22 | **Bernhard Wilhelm**, Paris | *Bernhard Wilhelm*, 2001 |
| 23 | **Bernhard Wilhelm**, Paris | *man with iron*, 2001 |
| 24 | **Richie Hawtin**, Ontario | *Richie Hawtin, home, sitting*, 1994 |
| 25 | **Bobby Gillespie**, London | *Bobby Gillespie*, 1991 |

1 **Irm Hermann** 2000

2 **Valerie Villaume** 2000

3 **Richard James** 2001

5 **Markus Krottendorfer** 1998

6 **Andre Weisheit** 2000

7 **Billie Ray Martin** 1999

9  **Hedi Slimane**  2000

10 **Volker Antenreiter** 2000

11 **Jochen Klein** 1997

12 **Jason Evans** 2000

13 **Wolfgang Tillmans** 1997

14 **Morwenna Banks** 1995

15 **Grandmaster Flash** 1995

16 **Jarvis Cocker** 1998

17 **Michael Clark** 1998

18  **Chris Cunningham** 1998

19  **Vidya Gastaldon**  1999

20  **Chloe Sevigny** 1995

21 **Steve Slocombe** 1999

23  **Bernhard Wilhelm** 2001

24  **Richie Hawtin** 1994

25 **Bobby Gillespie** 1991

26 **Alexandra Bircken Faridi** 1997

27 **Michael Stipe** 1997

28 **Rachel Auburn & Jack** 1995

29 **Wolfgang Tillmans** 1988

30 **Donald Cameron** 2000

31 **Anatoli Karpow** 1999

32 **Elisabeth Tillmans** 1994

33 **Smokin' Jo** 1995

34 **Käthe Gilles** 2000

35 **Bianca Jagger** 1998

36  **Elisabeth Peyton**  1995

37 **Jason Evans** 1994

38 **Richard James** 1993

39 **Jochen Klein** 1995

40 **Frank Terhardt** 2000

41 **Alison Folland** 1995

42 **Arnd Kegel** 1991

43 **Arnd Kegel** 1991

44 **Bother Arnold** 1995

45 **Brother Hugh** 2000

46 **John Waters** 1996

47 **John Waters** 1996

49  **Barnaby Wallace** 1991

51 **Paula Hayes & Rylan Morrison** 1995

53 **Adam Shepard** 1991

54 **St. Etienne** 1991

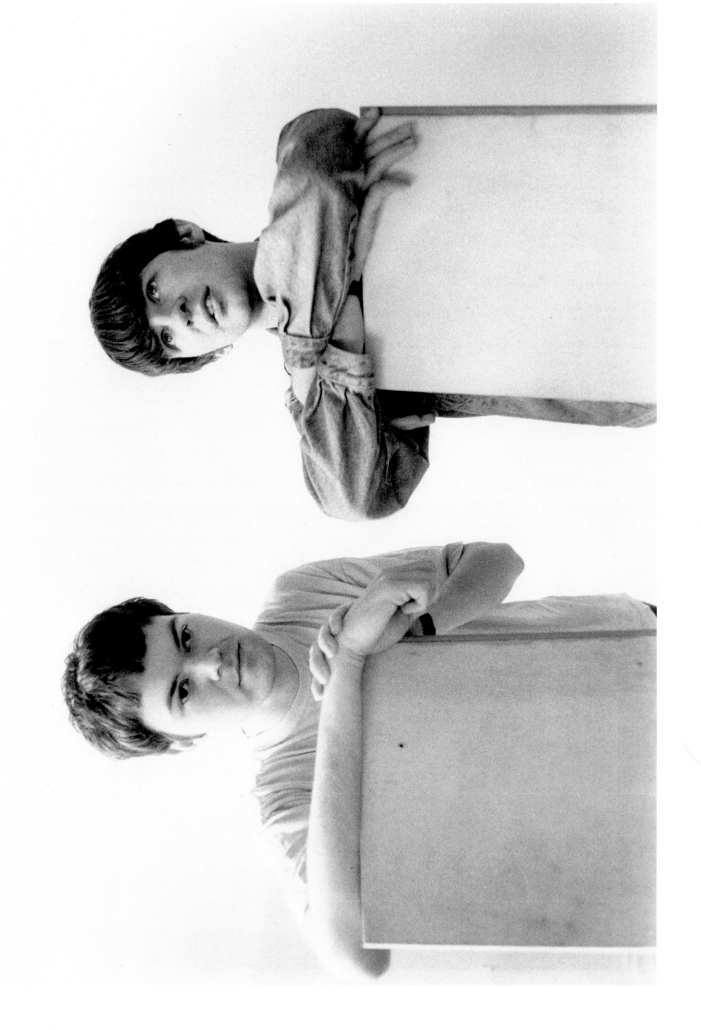

56 **Isa Genzken** 1993

57 **Isa Genzken** 1995

58 **Isa Genzken** 1999

59 **Mark Loy** 1998

60 **Lutz Huelle** 1998

61 **Simon de Pury** 2001

63  **Gillian Wearing** 1996

64  **Alex James & Damon Albarn** 1995

65 **Michael Imperioli** 2001

66 **Jarvis Cocker** 1998

67 **Carmen Brunner** 2001

68 **Supergrass** 1997

© 2001 Wolfgang Tillmans and Verlag der

Buchhandlung Walther König, Cologne

*Conception:* Wolfgang Tillmans

*Cover typography:* Scott King

*Typesetting:* Silke Fahnert, Uwe Koch, Cologne, Germany

*Lithography:* SK Litho, Lohmar, Germany

*Printing:* Druckerei Uhl, Radolfzell, Germany

ISBN 3-88375-535-4